C000253950

The One-Week Budget

Get One Step Closer to Financial Freedom by Creating an Easy Money Management System That Will Help You Make More Money and Keep You Debt Free

Volume 2

By

Income Mastery

© **Copyright 2020- All rights reserved.**

The following book is written with the goal of providing information as accurate and reliable as possible. In any case, the purchase of this book considers that both the publisher and the author are not experts in the topics covered and that the recommendations or suggestions made here are for entertainment purposes only. Professionals should be consulted as necessary before undertaking any of the actions mentioned here.

This statement is considered fair and valid by both the American Bar Association and the Committee of the Publishers Association and is considered legal throughout the United States.

In addition, the transmission, duplication or reproduction of any of the following works, including specific information, shall be considered an illegal act regardless of whether it is in electronic or printed form. This extends to the creation of a secondary or tertiary copy of the work or a recorded copy and is only permitted with the express written consent of the author. All additional rights reserved.

The information on the following pages is generally considered to be a truthful and accurate description of the facts and, as such, any lack of attention, use or misuse of the information in question by the reader will cause the resulting actions to be solely within his or her competence. There are no scenarios in which the publisher or author of this book can be held responsible for any difficulties or damages that may occur to them after making the information presented here.

In addition, the information on the following pages is intended for informational purposes only and should therefore be regarded as universal. As befits its nature, it is presented without warranty with respect to its prolonged validity or provisional quality. The trademarks mentioned are made without written consent and can in no way be considered as sponsorship of the same.

Table of Contents

Develop proper money management

It's important that you develop the right money management skills, with calculations and basic financial knowledge so that you can avoid falling into bankruptcy, or simply being heavily indebted even to the person who sells the newspapers on the block. You can take the following steps to develop proper money management:

- **Set priorities:** basic consumer spending is not flexible. In this case it is important to consider basic expenses such as food, health, consumption of water, electricity, gas, transportation, condominium, telephone and internet (if you work with him), minimum quality of life needs. Once this aspect has been addressed, it is essential to establish investment priorities, according to the opportunities and financial capacity in all senses, such as the availability of resources, debt option, possibilities of alliances and partnerships, capacity to pay on time, among others.

- **Don't be afraid to get into debt:** credit is a very important option for supporting people's progress, as we mentioned earlier. Be honest with the information you provide to the entity that will study your ability to pay, because this way you can establish an objective and realistic limit which you can meet your ability to pay, without affecting or drowning in rough debts that then you cannot pay. As far as possible, it uses credit only for projects that generate returns, increase capital or strengthen its productive capacity. Avoid using credit as much as possible for unnecessary consumer expenses or luxuries.

- **Distribute your money rationally:** it is important to establish the amount of your income that will be allocated to meet each of your needs and commitments and make the payment dates coincide with those of his salary to avoid arrears and interest cost overruns on arrears. Do not forget that it is always necessary to think about unforeseen events and contingencies. For contingencies, it is important to create an emergency fund to save any contingency that may arise.

- **Don't be afraid to disinvest** evaluate the opportunity to leave your investments at the right time or at the highest value. For example, if you have a property, analyze the possible development that the place may have, and do not discard its sale to use the money in another investment more profitable and equally safe. For this, you must manage a good investment plan, with a step-by-step of what to do to make it work.

- **Don't buy on impulse:** make sure that all your expenses are justified and of great importance, that is, if they are not vital, try not to make them, and save that money for more vital issues such as meals, house payments, transportation, health, etc. Any expense must have a minimum of support within the rationale of personal financial management.

- **Invest or save in education**: many studies show that the basic saving, and the most productive added value of a country, a community, a family or an individual, is education, understood as the accumulation of knowledge at the service of progress and development through productive projects. It is an added value of all communities, political trends, and much more, that help shape the way people live, always looking for the best for the person. Allocating resources to boost production capacity is fundamental in the strategy of successfully managing money at a personal or family level.

- **Do not spend more than you earn**: although this may sometimes seem a little difficult, you should be careful not to overspend your budget. Think: if you spend more money than you receive, how will you repay the debt? If you answered "borrowing", you would be borrowing a lot more, and doubling the level of difficulty getting out of debt. It is key to establish the difference between expenditure and investment: the former does not bring economic return, while the latter does, which implies that a person can increase his income by managing his money well. Only when this happens will it be possible to increase spending on other matters.

- **Economize**. The sacrifices you make today may result in benefits later.

- **Learn to distinguish between luxury and necessity.** Don't confuse needs with desires. The people who save the most, limit the purchases that are just for fun. They prefer to save with a view to achieving economic stability rather than spending on current tastes or luxuries, superficial things and luxuries.

- **Study your habits and routines.** Many people have at least one expensive habit. It can be an ordinary coffee or a cappuccino that is drunk every day, the craving for new shoes or the habit of going out to dinner. Study all your habits and routines to see what you can cut back on, so you don't spend more than you have and even have some money to save.

- **Avoid impulse purchases**. When the idea of acquiring something unforeseen comes up, give yourself a few days to think if you really need it. It's a good idea to follow the 3-day rule, which is that for all major purchases, wait three days before deciding, enough days for your enthusiasm to wane and reason to intervene, making sure that the purchase is the best option.

- **Pay with cash or debit card**. Research has shown that people are more likely to spend when they buy with a credit card, but when you want to pay with your own money, you think twice so as not to squander your monthly budget. So, if you want to control your expenses more, consider paying cash.

- **Visualize yourself reaching your goals**. If you're trying to raise a contingency fund, save money for a specific need, or even save to give yourself an unusual taste, every time you come up with the idea of making a purchase or making a decision that means spending money, think about the economic goal you've set for yourself. If the purchase in question is not going to bring you closer to your goal, ask yourself if you can do without it.

- **Enjoy the simple and free.** In life there are so many things to delight in that don't cost money. Explore and enjoy the simple, and you'll see how remarkable and enriching certain shared activities and experiences can be that are literally priceless. For example, a walk in the park, outings to the mall, family plans, among others.

- **Make a short- and medium-term personal or family budget:** this should include consumption expenses, savings portion (preferably productive), entertainment, vacations and unforeseen expenses. When it is a family budget, individual responsibilities can be assigned, according to the income of each of the members of the group, either by contributing a specific monthly amount of money or by indicating the commitment assumed by each person. For example, utilities, credit repayment, leasing, study, food, etc.

- **Save**: the money you can receive today is part of the money you'll have tomorrow. It is important to point out that there are various forms of savings, and that the most profitable is that of productive savings, that is, savings made to generate new income, in such a way that they not only conserve the value of what has been saved but also increase capital. Examples: education, housing and valuables. Don't forget that old age is an unassailable reality. Contribute to your pension. To apply for this type of savings, it is important that you have a minimum of preparation to develop it correctly.

- **Be clear about the difference between spending and investment**: spending is that activity that involves the outflow of money with no economic return. Some of the expenditures produce returns represented in happiness and quality of life, but these should only be made when general economic circumstances permit.

Remember that the investment is one whose main objective is to generate a return, where you can receive a number of dividends free of expenses.

- **When it comes to investing** get the best possible advice. Although the investment is intended to generate a return, a bad decision can put you at risk and cause the opposite effect. Don't concentrate your investments on a single option, unless you're just starting the dynamic. Diversification is a way to reduce exposure to risk.

- **Do not exceed the limit of indebtedness**: unless the money you borrow is to take advantage of or undertake in a business that generates good dividends and good profitability (cost-opportunity), avoid indebtedness. Financial institutions consider that, on average, an individual or family should not be indebted to more than 30 percent of their fixed income, as this can cause an imbalance in their economy and bring problems.

Following these recommendations will help you respect and take better care of your money, as well as manage your debts correctly. A debt-free person is a happy person because he or she is not accountable to anyone, has no financial commitments to make, and mentally allows you to think of new and better financial growth strategies for yourself.

What are SMEs?

SMEs are small and medium-sized enterprises that seek their financial independence, following the examples of the large national and transnational corporations of each country. They are independent companies that seek to establish a place in the trade market, being excluded from the industrial market because they do not have large investments, which characterize the industrial market. For this reason, an SME will never be able to exceed certain annual sales or a certain number of staff.

SMEs are a great strategy to get out of debt without having to become big investors, and for that, you can follow the following tips (with reference information from the portal Buenos Negocios):

Seven keys to developing SMEs with friends

Running a small or medium business has a lot of responsibility, as much as running a mega corporation, so it is important and advisable to run a business with friends who are experts in strategic areas within the company. To develop an SME, you must:

1. **Have (and maintain) joint objectives.** There are countless reasons why someone starts a business. In addition to money and economic

aspects, drivers such as personal development, growth possibilities, global problem solving, time flexibility, fame, among others, tend to be added. If you're going to start a business with friends, it's essential to talk about each one's expectations. What are they looking for? What would be the "ideal business" model for each one? What do they want to prioritize? What do they imagine in a few years? What do they consider "success" or "failure" of the business? Once underway, doing at least an annual review of these questions will allow the team to keep aligned or adjust as necessary, without accumulating tensions that may affect the day to day.

2. **"Clear beads..."** While it may not be the main driver for some entrepreneurs, money is always a central part of any project. To preserve friendship, it is essential to be orderly and talk about economic and financial issues: what and how each will contribute to the initial investment of the business, what income they will have, who will handle the money, and so on. It is not only a matter of making informal agreements, but also of reflecting this in formal aspects, such as the composition of the society, the possession of goods and the participation in profits (and losses). If they do not have experience or specialized training, an accountant can help organize these aspects.

3. **Are we all replaceable?** One of the theoretical principles of organizations is that all people can be replaced. However, when a group of friends starts a business it is partly because they want to work with their group of membership, and this can be one of their differentiators from their competitors: teams that already know each other tend to work better and are more motivated to overcome natural obstacles in starting and growing a business.

4. **Establish a "friendship protocol".** Just as well-managed family businesses have a family protocol that establishes the rules of operation in the face of the complexity of the work and family relationship, something similar can be done between friends. We recommend that you prepare a document with some basic guidelines that can serve as a guide in difficult situations in the company (entry of partners, distribution of responsibilities, conflict resolution mechanisms, sale of the business, etc.). Talking with time and without pressure on these issues then facilitates decisions and avoids frictions that could damage the friendship.

5. **Emotions versus efficiency.** Don't let one of the characteristics influence more than the other, that is, if there are more emotions than efficiency, the business won't have the maturity to advance, and if it has more efficiency than

emotion, you won't have time to feel and know what your business needs to improve. The two dimensions must coexist in a delicate balance so that business does not stagnate, or friendship deteriorates.

6. "Mentor, coach, therapist, organizational psychologist, consultant... Searching for someone outside the business to help maintain "difficult conversations" can be a way to facilitate the relationship and decision making.

7. **Enjoy the day to day.** Find ways to take advantage of the work environment to nurture friendship and have fun: lunches, meetings, business trips, New Year's Eve parties, among others.

The idea of getting together among friends to form business strategies is that they can have fun and grow together in a joint project.

Now, we cannot forget another great strategy to apply in the development of an SME and refers to the practice of using electronic checks. The digital world is advancing, and companies are forced to apply changes and updates to their platforms and ways of working in order not to become obsolete in their different markets. Digital checks can greatly facilitate a company's banking and financial operation.

Like wire transfers, electronic checks are a great tool, because you no longer need paper money to exchange goods and do business, something that is becoming unnecessary for people.

According to the Buenos Negocios portal, the new electronic checks, or Echeqs, entered into force in Argentina in July 2019, following Central Bank regulations. These are electronic documents circulating only through digital channels and constituting payment orders from an issuer with a current account at a bank, so that a legitimate recipient or bearer can cash the amount detailed in the cheque. Although their use is not mandatory for the time being, they are expected to gradually replace the physical cheque, with the same legal backing.

Like traditional cheques, Echeqs are issued from current accounts, although they can also be deposited for collection at savings banks, and pay the tax on bank credits and debits, as recently specified by AFIP. Initially, they can only be cashed by bankers, depositing them in their accounts, although it is expected that in the future, they may also be cashed over the counter like some paper checks.

Among its advantages, it is possible to emphasize that:

- The issuance, endorsement, negotiation and general circulation operations are simplified, as all these steps are carried out through digital channels (they are broadcast and "signed" through electronic banking).

- Checks have no limits on the number of endorsements, that is, third-party checks can be used to make payments and be transferred to different recipients.

- They have a lower operating cost than traditional checks, as they reduce the need to move and verify documents.

- They are safer and more effective by reducing the likelihood of counterfeiting, adulteration or the loss or theft of checkbooks.

- Many of the reasons for rejecting checks are reduced, especially those related to formal aspects (such as erroneous account numbers, illegible information, date errors, etc.).

- As they are easier to negotiate and verify, it is simpler to use them as a form of financing, through the assignment or sale of documents.

Once this strategy is developed and understood, we embark on the 8 keys to manage payments. This management helps us to reduce many financial commitments such as payroll payment to your employees, your suppliers, and any other creditor of the company. As the company grows, the activities and amounts to be paid for operations and everything related to the maintenance of the company increase, something that can generate headaches if it is not paid on time and if a suitable financial and work model is not developed so that it works automatically. Payments are a central aspect of the operational wheel of any business and, in order to make them efficiently, it is necessary to follow some good practices:

- Consider your payments as a key aspect of your financial planning. Keep track of your commitments and operations, track and analyze data, and make informed decisions.

- Select the most efficient payment method for each case. There are many ways to make payments, each with different risks, costs and practicality: checks, deposits and bank transfers, payment services to suppliers, payment to collectors, cash. Evaluate the legal requirements and usual practices in your area and sector to decide the best form of payment in each case.

- Sets a payment schedule. Even if you handle few operations, it is easier to devote one day per week or fixed schedule to the management of payments.

- Manages one or more small boxes for minor or unforeseen expenses.

- Keep your cash flow up to date, to anticipate money needs or surpluses. Be clear about the difference between perceived and accrued criteria. In particular, schedule payment dates for issued checks to avoid the costs of rejected checks.

- Avoid the hidden costs of thinking only in the short term. It's not about plugging holes and going out to get money when you have to pay. For a comprehensive financial analysis, especially in a context of inflation, you need to consider the generation of interest on delinquencies on outstanding invoices and the cost of borrowing if you are going to use the bank overdraft to make payments.

- Think beyond money. Payments are often a key aspect of the relationship with employees, suppliers and others, and therefore their timely compliance can impact more than financially. Prioritize the payment of wages and salaries to keep your team motivated, pay your key suppliers first and be sure to consider the impact of your decisions on your future relationship.

- Internal control. Managing the money that goes out of business is a sensitive aspect; be sure to take the basic steps to avoid out-of-control and temptations. For example, it separates the tasks of preparing payments from those of moving money; it performs surprise arcades and rotates the staff who handle the money. A consultant or your accountant can help you set up safe circuits and establish control mechanisms.

It is very important to maintain control and care in all the businesses you wish to undertake or start developing. A constant monitoring of all the procedures of your company will allow you to foresee an unforeseen event and correct it in time, or simply avoid it, so that when you act on the matter, it is no longer too late. You must consider that creating your own business will not make you a millionaire quickly, unless you win the lottery, but that would not be entrepreneurship, but chance, so you must have patience to begin to see the great results of it. This is an overview of the main personal finance concepts you should consider, especially if you are an entrepreneur:

- **Your starting point conditions you.** Some come to their own business with ample personal and family funds, while others come only with their talent, enthusiasm and good ideas. In any case, it is true that there are entrepreneurs who start with nothing, and go very far, while others with huge investments like that do not find success. However, the initial finances impact not only on how much personal money you can invest in the business but also on the level of risk you can assume and the support you have in case of need or failure.

- **For entrepreneurs it is even more difficult to have an accurate diagnosis of personal finances.** With a little order, a worker in a dependency relationship can be clear about how much he generates and how much he spends, how much he contributes to his retirement and how much he is retained monthly for social work and other benefits. For an independent worker or business owner, on the other hand, accounts are not that simple. It's easy to lose control with so much going on around you: money tied up in business assets or working capital, irregular entrepreneurial income, business debts and commitments, money from partners and investors, and even large sums circulating even when the business is not profitable. It is vital to make periodic evaluations to know how much personal money you really have, and how much of that may be available in case of need. An accountant can advise you if you have any doubts.

- **Separate (and ordered) accounts reduce risks.** On the one hand, it tries to separate the accounts of the business from those of its owner, because sometimes they tend to mix in the day to day. This involves not only keeping the register independently but ensuring that the business is formally constituted as an entity separate from its owners. On the other hand, if there is more than one partner or if it is a family business, it is necessary to be ordered to reflect reality. It is common, for example, for some commercial goods to be placed in the name of family members, or for family members to use a company vehicle or spend money on behalf of the business. As long as everything flows, maybe nothing happens. But at some critical personal (e.g. divorce) or business (e.g. labor lawsuit) moment, disorder can pay dearly.

- **Align expectations and reality**. Some look for a way to earn a lot of money in their own business, others focus on creating a job that they like and that gives them freedom. Some seek to revolutionize the world, while others measure recognition only in economic results. Working as a family, having flexible hours or making your own decisions are some of the additional benefits of self-employment. Being clear about what you are looking for in entrepreneurship and what you want to receive in return, putting everything in the balance, will help you to enjoy your entrepreneurial path.

- **The extra effort of women entrepreneurs.** Women who choose to turn to their own business often face additional barriers in addition to the challenges typical of any entrepreneur. Access to financial education and personal money management are some of the most recent challenges on the road to gender equity.

- **Everyone who undertakes it hopes that it will go well,** however, is not the reality for many, so not only must be mentally prepared to overcome the failure, but also must organize the accounts to be able to move forward in case of need. The general recommendation, for entrepreneurs and non-entrepreneurs, is to maintain a readily available reserve fund, with money to survive at least six months without income. It will allow you to reorganize and try again or get a job in the meantime.

- **Managing growing wealth is also a challenge**. An additional tip if you have the luck and ability to be among those who through your own business come to wealth, is to learn to manage your wealth and manage it so that you can maximize the growth of your business and your personal development.

A good strategy to guarantee your financial future with your ventures is to follow all the strategies mentioned above. But if your business operates a point of sale to accept debit and credit cards, it's critical to know what chargebacks are, why they can be generated, and how to claim to recover the money from that sale when possible.

A chargeback is a debit that the administrator or financial entity of the credit card makes to the merchant on a transaction that had already been paid and arises from a claim of the issuing bank or the cardholder in question.

The characteristics of a chargeback are as follows:

- **Countercharges for lack of knowledge of purchase:** it happens when the client says he did not make that purchase, it can happen because he does not recognize the operation in the summary of the bank. There are measures that trade can take to avoid chargebacks for this reason.

- **Rejections: the** operation was not accepted by the card, for some error the purchase was not processed. To retrieve these coupons, the only option is to contact the customer. This is why it is essential to have your data.

- **Return: a** customer made a purchase; the card was paid for and then the customer requested the return. In these cases, the card makes a chargeback for return.

- **Chargeback for duplicate sales:** if for some reason the card receives the same coupon twice, it generates a chargeback for one of them. If both have been processed from the POS terminal and both are signed by the customer, the card holder must pay them and both charges are made.

- **Promotional chargeback:** when a bank arranges a promotion with the trade and pays the full sale, it makes a promotional chargeback to discount what they had agreed to. These chargebacks are not claimable.

But this should not worry you, because here we will recommend three strategies to avoid chargebacks:

1. **Always ask for the document next to the card and check the data.** The main tool available to the trade to claim a chargeback is the signed coupon. That's why you should always ask for the document next to the card and check the data, that the photo matches the person who is making the purchase and that the signature of the card and the coupon are not very different. In the latter case, it is preferable to cancel the coupon and reprint it for the customer to sign again. You can also help avoid chargebacks by having the merchant record the customer's document and phone number, rather than asking the customer to write it down. This way the trade is sure to understand the letter and not lose the data.

2. **Trying to make the company name and fantasy name similar.** One of the most common reasons for refusals is the difficulty in associating the fantasy name of the trade with the business name that appears on credit card statements. Whenever possible, the name next to which the customer is going to observe the amount of the purchase in the summary, should be equally or easily related to that of the trade.

3. **Products in good condition and friendly customer service.** The third key has to do with people's experience in commerce. Customer service is extremely important in many respects, even to avoid chargebacks. Also, the quality of the products and the state in which they are stored. The control of stock (quantity of goods) helps to optimize these resources and that customers leave the premises satisfied. When this does not happen, they may be unaware of purchases as a form of protest and, if they do not have the documentation mentioned above, they lose time and money.

What to do and how to react to a chargeback?

As recommended by the Buenos Negocios agency, specialized in business finance, from the day the commerce receives the liquidation, it has a period of time to make any type of claim that depends on each credit card.

After that time, the settlement is considered consensual and any right to challenge is lost and there will no longer be any way to recover the money debited from the sale that suffered the chargeback. It is fundamental that the commerce controls the sales with cards to find out in time of the chargebacks of your business and to be able to make the claims every time that corresponds, this is the most advisable thing to carry out the claim, which varies according to each card. Step one is to locate the coupon signed by the customer and scan it.

Already developed all the strategies to undertake in an SME, it is also important to plan well in advance your retirement or retirement, because obviously you do not want to work or be at the forefront of your business for life, although perhaps at this time say yes, when the time comes you might regret that thinking.

Therefore, some actions you can take right now to start planning that big step, even if you prefer not to think about leaving your venture, are:

- **Register and pay contributions with your future in mind.** You can't just count on an official retirement to fund retirement years. Although the payment of self-employed workers, and the payment of monotax to a lesser extent, imply contributions that count for calculating future retirements in the state system, generally these are amounts of retirements that are going to be significantly lower than the usual income of an entrepreneur, and that of their peers in a relationship of dependency. In many cases, moreover, entrepreneurs work in the informal sector without making such contributions, and therefore have difficulty accessing the system. Find out your situation with an accountant: years of contributions, retirement you could access, registration options to improve your future income, and so on.

- **Separate personal and business money.** A common mistake of many entrepreneurs is to mix individual or family goods and money with those belonging to the commercial activity. Put all the accounts in order, this represents a great step to understand with how much accounts for retirement, or to know the value of the business in case of sale or transfer.

- **Estimate retirement needs and financial possibilities.** How much money will you need per month when you are no longer working?

What would you like to do in retirement years? What part can come from retirement and what part from savings or liquidation of assets? Think that to your normal expenses and projected activities you will probably have to add medical and care expenses, as well as expenses that today you can have covered from the business. If projected accounts don't close, be sure to start saving to make the future you envision a reality.

- **Put together a business retirement plan**. It's not just about doing the math; it's also important to establish the steps you're going to take to leave the business: what role do you want, and can you keep? When would you like to leave the activity? What happens if you get sick and are forced to leave the business unexpectedly?

- **Plan the succession, transfer or sale of the business**. Some entrepreneurs choose to always be close to their business and keep working, while others prefer to put an end to and enjoy retirement free of work-related occupations. In both cases it is necessary to prepare it is not easy to organize the succession of the family business, the transfer to a third party or the sale of a business or goodwill.

If you have a successful financial history and believe it's time for your business to jump-start and grow, it's time to know how much money you could earn through credit that helps you maximize your wealth. Credit, if well used, can be a growth engine for small and medium-sized enterprises. These are not only loans, but there are various forms of financing offered by financial system institutions, such as corporate cards and account overdrafts.

If you want to apply for a loan, you must take into account a number of factors, because, on the one hand, those who lend the money evaluate some formal aspects, for example, how your company is legally constituted, who are its partners and what is the history of the company. On the other hand, aspects related to the development of the business are considered, such as, for example, how you are going to apply the money ordered and how your projections improve due to the use of credit.

You should consider the following scenarios, based on the requirements usually requested by local banks, to understand how much credit and what type of credit you can access, depending on the stage of business your company is in:

1. **Start-up companies.** There are some lines of credit to promote the formation of new companies, although it is not easy to obtain formal loans for businesses that do not show a certain trajectory. Check if your project meets the necessary requirements to qualify for these incentives.

2. **Companies that are not formally incorporated**. Lack of formality or independent registration are often barriers to obtaining business financing. You can get money in the form of personal loans, which are usually more expensive than those oriented toward formally incorporated businesses.

3. **Individuals with commercial activity.** Some professionals, traders and service providers of a certain size may have a significant turnover, even if they operate under a registration as natural persons. This usually entitles them to special lines of credit, which may include credit cards, overdrafts and loans that may be backed by pledges or require certain guarantees.

4. **Formally constituted companies, with basic file.** If your company is a SA (corporation) or SRL (limited liability company) only with minimal documentation and meeting certain background requirements, it is possible to receive basic financing in the form of overdraft agreements, purchase of corporate checks and credit cards. For this purpose, the presentation of the copy of the last balance sheet, the social contract or statute, the powers granted by the company, the acts of appointment of authorities, among other requirements that will depend on the financial entity where you will apply for credit. As for the background, the credit history

is evaluated, in particular, that there are no delinquent debts in other banks, or have pension debt, or tax executions in force, among other aspects.

5. **Formally incorporated companies, with complete documents.** If you can add more balances (two previous years minimum), to the information and background of the previous point evolution of sales, projections of the business with and without financing, and other documents that show a solid case, you will have access to a better rating that allows you to receive more money. To the instruments mentioned in the previous point, fully rated companies may have access to financial loans, in some cases for specific purposes, such as equipment.

If you already have a business, it's important to control card sales, even if it's a complex task. Some of the reasons that can make this activity difficult are the following:

- It is important to log in every day to download the settlement and review chargebacks.

- Liquidations are often not friendly or easy to understand.

- To make use of the data you need to manually pass it to Excel.

For this reason, experts indicate that lack of control over card payments is very common. Many card merchants do not have visibility into their cash flow, which is one of the main indicators of the merchant's financial condition. This affects trade because it prevents it from planning. It is essential to have projected revenues and expenditures on hand to make better decisions and to know the real possibilities of meeting payment commitments or to know how an investment will impact cash flow projection.

You can lose a lot of money for these situations:

- **Rejections and chargebacks that are not claimed on time**: chargebacks are debits that administrators make on operations that have already been paid. In some cases, they can be claimed, but if the trade doesn't know it and doesn't do it in time it loses that money.

- **Delays in accreditation:** due to lack of control, merchants may not perceive a delay in the deposits they must receive for their credit and debit card sales. Any error in this process is difficult to see without the right tools.

- **Loss of money due to unclear cash flow**: many businesses advance payments because they are uncertain about the amounts that will be credited to their accounts or about the deadlines.

This generates financial costs that can be avoided.

- **Non-Recoverable Withholding**: A percentage of the cost of card sales is tax and withholding. If this amount is accounted for correctly, it can be recovered, and the tax credit maximized. Lack of clarity causes businesses to lose sight of it, not process it correctly, and then it becomes a cost they could avoid.

For this reason, experts suggest using a tool to automate this complex process of card sales control, and thus have accurate information taken from the card administrators and ordered to have a clear picture of the money that will come from sales each day, without the need to re-check coupons by hand.

Common mistakes made during the use of money

Many people make countless mistakes when it comes to using money, which means that at the end of the month they are very short of it, however, if you take into account and become aware of these errors, you can control and use your money in a more effective way.

A study conducted by the Intersectoral Commission for Economic and Financial Education in Colombia found that these are the most common mistakes people make when handling their money:

- 94% of respondents reported that they planned their budget, but only 23% knew exactly when they had spent the previous week.

- 88% of adults expressed concern about having to face higher expenses in the future (e.g. retirement).

- Only 41% have plans to pay for their old-age expenses, and only 1 in 5 could afford the significant unforeseen expenses.

- Those consulted have high scores in the knowledge of simple economic and financial concepts, but a smaller proportion have correct answers in the estimation of the simple or compound interest rate, or on the knowledge of bank deposit insurance, which are concepts that eventually allow better financial decisions to be made.

- People have a high orientation to the present, for example, they say "I'd rather spend money than save for the future", a popular phrase among savers.

- In terms of expenditure control and savings, approximately 60% of all adults carry a budget, control their expenditure and save on a daily basis, although most do so outside the financial system.

Once some of the main mistakes made by people have been detected, you can follow a series of recommendations to improve your financial status. Among the recommendations are:

- **Make a budget**: you should have a clear relationship of how much money goes into your pocket and how much you are spending. If you manage household accounts, you should be very responsible for the money you put in and what you're getting into. There can be no waste, and for that, it is useful to classify it in items such as education, housing, entertainment and transportation, among others.

- **Learn to say 'NO'**: many times, an occasional outing, a birthday, a social celebration represents a monetary quota that was not counted in the monthly, weekly or daily budget. Then the best thing is to say, "for next time" or "this time I can't".

- **Get out of debt:** when there is no income and bills are overdue, the solution to illiquidity is to borrow from someone. If you are forced into debt, remember to have additional income to pay your obligations. That way you'll save money and disgust.

- **Invest:** Once you've accumulated some money from your savings, it's time to put them to work.

- **Plan**: In most cases, we can identify income and expenses that are approaching, either short-term, such as job bonuses or Christmas gifts, or long-term, such as retirement. Establish a financial plan for these events, don't leave it to chance or to last minute.

- **Paying on time:** being 'good pay' is your best letter of introduction in the financial system, do not leave the payment of your public or private bills for the last day, as this habit makes you more likely to go into default or fall behind with your obligations.

- **Protect:** no one has the future bought, look for mechanisms that help minimize the economic impacts of fortuitous situations such as earthquakes, traffic accidents or disease.

- **Acquire financial education**: empower yourself with your relationship to the financial system and understand how it can support you in achieving your goals.

Your way of thinking must change to avoid the financial hemorrhages in your life, because with these recommendations you can stop and avoid many economic problems with families, providers, and more. If you are still not convinced of these techniques, we recommend 5 simple steps to get out of debt:

1. **Mentality.** That thought that makes you feel an emotion that leads you to act in a certain way and get a result. Simply decide to buy your freedom by getting out of debt and act accordingly.

2. **Keeps a Record of Expenses.** In order to get rid of your loans and credit cards, you may need to improve and control your personal finances. You have to know how much you make and what you spend it on. If you have to save to use that money (or part of it) to get out of debt, you will have to know exactly on which items you spend the money. Write down your expenses and once a month analyze where your money has gone, this will allow you to make concrete and accurate decisions about which expenses you are going to reduce or do without to reach your goal of ending your debts.

3. **He scores and orders**. Write down all your debts, and not just your bank debts, for example,

if a relative of yours ever lent you money, if you owe any term of a purchase of greater amount, write them on a sheet and put it somewhere visible, this will allow you to be focused on your goal. If you add a photograph of something you want to do (a trip, for example) once you get out of debt, your motivation will be strengthened.

4. **Act**. It orders the debts of the previous item by time from lowest to highest. The ones you have the least time left to finish will be the first you must attack. Allocate the monthly savings you make after detecting money leaks in step 2 with your spending control and dedicate that amount to paying off the debt that appears first on your list in advance. When you're done with it, use the monthly savings plus the installment of the finished debt and go for debt number 2 on your list. Cancel debt number 2 on your list early with that money.

5. **Accelerates the process with extra income**. If it is a common and current income of those who exchange your time for money (on behalf of others or as self-employed) does not work, because you would fall into the paradox of being even more slave, the ideal is that you implement a passive income, the one you want.

Boost your debt-free living strategy

You can live with the philosophy of living debt free. It is preferable that you live inhibiting yourself of luxuries, but calm and without debts, than spending more and suffering at the end of the month looking for the money to pay off your debts. To live debt free, you must follow these simple steps:

1. **Understand what kind of loans you have.** There are many ways to understand what a problem is, however, the first step in solving this will always be to define it. When we think about how to get out of debt, we usually do so out of the urgency of the day-to-day, the dissatisfaction with the feeling that you're only working to cover loan payments, or the anguish of living up to the thought of what juggling we'll do to make credit card payments this month, as we discussed earlier. If you really want to live without loans, the first thing you should do is have the broadest and clearest possible view of your financial situation to give it the urgency and importance it really requires. Doing so can be uncomfortable and generate fear and anxiety because it involves facing the result of many decisions you have made in the past consciously or unconsciously, but it will be a necessary encounter to have if

your deepest longing is to generate real change in the way we are managing our money and fulfilling our deepest objectives. Thus, the first step is to make a list as detailed as possible with the following information:

- **Who do I owe?** We are referring to the name of the person or to the name of the financial entity.

- **How much do I owe you?** In other words, the total value of the debt as of today. In other words, what you should pay him today if he wanted to wake you up tomorrow without that loan.

- **How much do I pay you each month?** In other words, the value of the share of the credit. If the fee is daily, weekly, or biweekly, just multiply it by the number of days, weeks, or fortnights in the month to find the total monthly payments you must make on that debt.

- **How long will it take for you to pay?** That is, the number of months remaining to leave that credit if you continued to pay your normal dues.

- **What effective annual interest rate do you charge me?** I mean, the percentage I have to pay every year to get that loan.

- **What would be a brief history of that debt?** What was the situation that encouraged or forced you to acquire that credit, and the decision process you followed to choose that loan?

2. Measure the impact these loans have on your personal finances

Not all loans have the same impact on your personal finances, in principle, because a consumer credit (credit card, free investment, etc.) is not comparable to a credit that was used for the purchase of long-term assets (mortgage or vehicle, for example), or against an informal credit (drop by drop, daily pay). Secondly, because there are credits with much higher quotas than others. Third, because they have different interest rates and annual costs, among others. Finally, because the habits that each of us has towards a debt end up conditioning their impact on our economy.

- **Assess your level of solvency:** When we talk about solvency, we mean the ability we have to meet our obligations based on the things we have, that is, what we want to know is whether the total value of our assets would be sufficient to cover our debts. As long as your total assets are higher than your total debts, you can say that you are financially solvent. However, when the value of your assets is less than the total of your debts, it can be said that you are not financially solvent.

- **Assess your level of liquidity**: In finance, when we talk about liquidity, we mean having enough cash to be able to meet the payments and obligations that we have to make on a day-to-day basis. Evaluating our liquidity level is very simple, for this, it is enough to compare the total value that we pay monthly in credit fees against our net income and our expenses. If you're too moderate or savvy when it comes to spending, it's possible that dividing your total installment payments by your total net income will result in a number greater than 0.3 (or 30%) indicating that you're facing liquidity problems.

Last but not least, Harvard University developed a fairly effective method of getting out of debt.

This method consists of prioritizing all debts with smaller balances, rather than focusing on obligations with higher interest rates. It seems a setback, because how is it better to pay the smallest balance and neglect those with the highest balance and higher interest rates?

According to the portal expansión.com, this is a system focused on reducing debt, both for individuals, natural person, as well as companies and businesses. The 'snowball method' was born from the research of several members of the Harvard Business Review.

For the methodology, an experiment was carried out in which several participants had to simulate the virtual payment of their debts. After obtaining the results, the authors of the study concluded that the factor that had the greatest impact was not the amount remaining to be paid, that is to say, the remaining debt, but the amount that they had managed to get rid of once paid.

If you analyze this conclusion, you probably infer that it makes more sense to pay bills with higher interest rates first, but you should think beyond that. People tend to be more confident and hopeful when they realize that part of their obligations are being eliminated no matter how small. In other words, focusing on paying off debts with lower interest rates tends to have a much more effective effect on the progress of total debt reduction.

How is the 'snowball method' used?

By decomposing Sall's spreadsheet, it is possible to use the method. It basically consists of:

- **Calculate economic capacity**: Help organize yourself with different Excel apps and templates to keep track of your income, expenses and debts. The greater the economic effort you make now to get rid of the debt, the less you will have to pay later, and therefore the sooner you will reach stability.

- **Plan:** Once you've done that, you have to figure out how much you can afford to spend on the higher debts. The idea is to see if you have the capacity to spend a greater amount each month to pay for them.

- **Pay:** You should write down and create a spreadsheet which includes all the debts you have, those that are smaller at the beginning and finally, the largest. It must include the interest rate for each of them and the minimum monthly payment for them. With this calculation you will see how many months you will have to dedicate to the payment of the debts until you manage to eliminate them completely.

Now, there are ten things you must do to get out of your debts, which are:

3. **Accept your debt**: Like any addiction, the first step to ending your addictions is to accept it. Therefore, you should begin by knowing the total amount of your debt and be determined to end it. To achieve this, you can do the following: write down and remember '**I'm going to get out of debt**', make a chart that allows you to see how much you are missing, share your situation with someone else, and don't try to hide it.

4. **Always negotiate your debt**: If you start negotiating in everything you do; it will be easier to save a good amount of money. In the case of debts, you can access entities that offer a portfolio purchase, this will help you lower interest, time payments and be more committed to the goal to achieve.

5. **Spend all your money to pay debts:** During a good time, you will have to make great sacrifices to be able to spend a larger amount for the payment of debts. Start by lowering the amount of luxury and unnecessary things you frequent in your life. You should also look for new income, with the goal of increasing your money and paying off the debt faster.

6. **Change your hobbies:** Try to leave the dependence on paid services like television, cell

phone plans and restaurants, and learn to appreciate what you have and what you really need. Do a study of what you really need and stay only with the basics, because saving a little money here can make a difference.

7. **Learn about money**: Spend time learning how to better manage your money. Today, there are a host of tools that will help you improve your financial health, including courses, conferences, expert assistance, counseling, and much more.

8. **Keep in mind the power of 'No'**: Remember you can always say no. Don't get involved in projects where you won't win something. Always make decisions that fit your plans and discard anything that won't do you any good. As well as saving on unnecessary expenses such as pay TV services, phone rents, and more, the money saved here will also be very helpful to you.

9. **Live with less**: Be more aware of what you really need to live and remember 'less is more'. Consumerism can be the best friend of financial institutions and the worst enemy of debtors, as they are increasingly indebted to financial institutions to pay those luxuries.

10. **Sell what's left over:** If you have items that you don't use and they're in good condition, sell them. This will help you earn extra income and meet the above goal.

11. **Use the cash to pay** If you are one of those who used the credit and you are in debt for it, better use the cash. This will help you put a realistic budget in place and limit yourself if you feel the need to overspend.

12. **Cook**: Eating out is really expensive. Therefore, try to prepare your food, you will see that your pocket and health will improve.

Conclusion

There are many factors that can positively and negatively influence your credit history, which can be fatal if you don't know how to use it to your advantage and can be very beneficial to you if you study every move well. As we say throughout this book, the main key is to avoid assuming debts that exceed the amount of your income, because logically you will not have how to pay off those debts in the future, and even worse, it will be very difficult to assume the costs of interest generated by the time the payment is late. If you are a person with financial intelligence, you will see that you can use this option in your favor, because you can apply for credits to create your own business or entrepreneurship that generates enough dividends to pay off your debts, and also generate that this money and business work for you, thus leaving the so difficult world of debts.

Correct all financial mistakes and bad vices that are part of your life by following the tips explained above. Avoid financial hemorrhaging, phantom expenses, such as continuing to pay for Gym membership, even if you don't go for lack of time, or you only go 2 days out of the 5 days you pay. You can lead a debt-free life with simple tips and strategies, plus measure the impact the loans you apply for make on your personal finances.

Now, if you are a person with a successful credit history, the bank will be the first one interested in increasing your credit limits so that you apply for them for use, but beware, because, although it may be beneficial for one party, it is a double-edged sword for the other. It is beneficial for the bank to increase your credit limits and for you to use them, because that generates more interest in favor of the financial entity, money that enters the bank for its maintenance, and that to tell the truth, that is the real business of the banks, but it can be dangerous for the applicant who is sometimes able to pay off, but may have other times where it is more complicated to do so, but if he uses it in a more intelligent way, as applying for loans to invest in his own business, or acquisitions that generate dividends, it can be very attractive and beneficial to him.

In summary, credits are a great strategy and financial tool used for the neediest, but also, for the entrepreneur who decides to devote himself to this business, the important thing is to participate in this in an intelligent way, with sufficient training and being advised by experts in the matter.

CPSIA information can be obtained
at www.ICGtesting.com
Printed in the USA
BVHW030914101022
649064BV00018B/618